Sir Thomas Browne: Amendments to the First

CW01024129

Since the first appearance of this booklet, twenty-three years ag
in the location of items described in the text. New informati
important amendments are as follows:

Chronology of the Life, Works and Skull of Sir Thomas Bro
cover (and on the Haymarket statue) of October 19th, was that g.... .. ..
Sir Thomas. St Michael-le-Querne parish registers were destroyed in the Great Fire, and only the year
of birth is given on his funeral monument in St Peter Mancroft. However, in a letter to Aubrey,
reproduced in the 1964 revision of Geoffrey Keynes' Works of Sir Thomas, Vol 4, p 374, Browne
states that he was born on November 19th, which is now accepted as the correct date.

Illustration number eight: The plaque depicted here was destroyed during rebuilding in the 1990's.
A new one, with revised wording, was placed at 11, The Haymarket, near the site of Browne's house.
Copies of an unpublished paper of 1999 by the author, titled Browne Plaques, are available in the
Library of Norwich Cathedral, and in The Norfolk Heritage Centre in the Norfolk and Norwich
Millennium Library at the Forum, Norwich.

Church of St Peter Mancroft: This section uses a record of the church published by the Rev. David
Sharp (vicar 1975-99), who produced a second, fuller version in 1994. This describes the Mancroft
Heritage Exhibition, a display of St Peter's treasures opened in the north transept in 1982. Six items
relating to Browne may be seen there, including the Gunton portrait, reproduced here as illustration
thirty-four.

Norwich Cathedral: This account of Browne's many associations with the Cathedral was produced
before the choice of items for an outstanding exhibition of Browniana, mounted in the Cathedral
Library for Browne 300, was made known to the author. The catalogue of this exhibition, which was
mounted by Anthony Beck, the assistant librarian, may be consulted in the Cathedral Library.

Wilkin Collection and Browne's Works: A major fire destroyed the City Library and Norfolk
Record Office in 1994. Fortunately, the Wilkin Collection and other works and manuscripts of Thomas
Browne, which were housed in them survived. Formerly accommodated in the same building as the
library, the Record Office is now located in the Archive Centre at County Hall, Martineau Lane,
Norwich, whilst the Local Studies Library, which used to be part of the City Library has now been
subsumed into the Norfolk Heritage Centre (see above). Many sources discussed in this booklet have
been affected by these moves.

Illustration twenty-two: The caption should read 'En sum: *See I am a burden which is lifted by five
fingers', from Browne's* Hydriotaphia or Urne Burial *(1658).*

Knighthood: This booklet presents the traditional account of Browne's knighthood, reputedly
conferred at the suggestion of the Mayor of Norwich, who had been in line for the honour. Recent
research suggests, however, that it was bestowed entirely in his own right: T. Hughes, *Norfolk
Archaeology*, 43 (1999), pp. 326-31.

Illustrations number thirty and thirty-one: The Norfolk and Norwich Hospital, St Stephen's Road,
Norwich, where the cast of Browne's skull depicted here was displayed, was closed in 2001 and
replaced by the newly built Norfolk and Norwich University Hospital at Colney, near the University of
East Anglia. Osler's casket was moved there, and is currently to be found in the new Sir Thomas
Browne library.

Browne's Norfolk: In the last part of this section, at the very end of the booklet, two examples of
memorials to Browne in Norwich are mentioned. The first concerns the medical library at the old
Norfolk and Norwich Hospital, which bore his name from 1978 onwards. A collection of books on the
medical history of Norfolk was also established in this library, and specifically known as 'the Sir
Thomas Browne Collection'. Both the Sir Thomas Browne Library and the Collection were moved to
the new hospital in 2001, and both names are still in use. The Thomas Browne Society of 1946, which
is also noted in the booklet, was disbanded before 1982 and its minutes may be consulted in the
Norfolk Record Office. Another local tribute to Browne dates from 1995, when the University of East
Anglia gave the name of 'The Thomas Browne Suite' to a group of rooms in its new Elizabeth Fry
Building.

Anthony Batty Shaw
Norwich 2005

Sir Thomas Browne of Norwich

Anthony Batty Shaw DM

'He was not a native of Norwich . . . but Norwich can look on him with pride as an adopted son, as one who elected to live the whole of his working life in this city; and who identified himself so absolutely with it, that his name is inseparable from it, and who will be known for all time as Sir Thomas Browne of Norwich.'
Sir Peter Eade (1894).

The Arms and Crest of Browne of Upton, Cheshire, as borne by Sir Thomas Browne.

'Doctor Thomas Brouneus · Ter bonus, cordatus homo' – an anagram sent to the then Dr Thomas Browne by Sir Philip Wodehouse of Kimberley, Norfolk (**3**, 274).

Second Impression, 2005
© Browne 2005 Committee
Norwich

Reprinted by Gutenberg Press

Originally published in 1982
Browne 300 Committee & Jarrold & Sons Ltd

Sir Thomas Browne of Norwich

''Tis opportune to look back upon old times, and contemplate our Forefathers. Great examples grow thin, and to be fetched from the passed world' (**1**, *132*).

Sir Thomas Browne, physician, philosopher and writer, was the greatest scholar and most original thinker to have lived within the city walls of Norwich. His enduring claims to fame rest on his reputation as one of the great writers of English prose, as a moralist and as a student of the philosophy of the seventeenth century in which he lived; familiar with six languages, a naturalist and antiquarian of distinction, Browne was the leading Norwich physician of his day and in his first and most celebrated work *Religio Medici* wrote on his own religious faith and its relation to his profession. However, while there is a large literature on Browne, no guide has so far been provided to his life in Norwich and his connections with its memorabilia. Such is the purpose of this memoir.

Life

'Nothing is more common with Infants than to dye on the day of their Nativity . . . but in Persons who out-live many Years, . . . that the first day should make the last, that the Tail of the Snake should return into its Mouth precisely at that time, and they should wind up upon the day of their Nativity, is indeed a remarkable Coincidence, which tho Astrology hath taken witty pains to salve, yet hath it been very wary in making Predictions of it. (**1**, *105*).

Browne was born in London in 1605. His father died when he was eight years of age and his mother later married Sir Thomas Dutton, a soldier and adventurer with estates in Ireland. In 1616 Browne was admitted as a scholar to Winchester College and in 1623 matriculated as a commoner of Broadgates Hall, Oxford, renamed Pembroke College during his second year there. After taking his MA in 1629 Browne visited his stepfather in Ireland and then, at a time when Oxford was not distinguished for its medical course, completed his medical studies abroad at Montpellier, Padua and Leiden where he proceeded MD in 1633. On returning to England there is debate as to whether he spent the next two years in medical practice at Shipden Vale, Yorkshire or in Oxfordshire but during these years he wrote *Religio Medici* though it was not published, and then in an anonymous and pirated edition, until 1642.

When he was thirty-one Browne moved to Norwich where he was to stay for the forty-six remaining years of his life. Norwich would have had its attractions for a young man intending to establish a practice as a physician for it was still the largest city of the realm after London, as it had been since the Norman Conquest. However, his main encouragement to settle in Norwich came from his former Oxford tutor, the Reverend Thomas Lushington who had moved to the city in 1635 as Chaplain to its Bishop, Richard Corbett, who had been Bishop of Oxford for the previous three years and before that Dean of Christ Church. He was also encouraged to settle in Norwich by three friends and contemporaries, two were sons of Norfolk families, Nicholas Bacon of Gillingham and Charles le Gros of Crostwight; the third Justinian Lewin, a fellow member of Pembroke College, was a barrister living in Heigham. Five years after his move to Norwich Browne married the daughter of another Norfolk family, Dorothy Mileham of North Burlingham (**2**).

Soon after he settled in Norwich Browne's first biographer recorded that he was much resorted to 'for his admirable skill in physick' and he established the leading medical practice of his day in East Anglia. In 1642, when Browne had been six years in Norwich, the Battle of Edgehill marked the outbreak of the Civil War when Browne, of Royalist sympathies, was to witness the Puritan sacking of the Cathedral and churches of Norwich. But apart from the disturbances of the Civil War and outbreaks of the plague his life in Norwich was a relatively quiet and uneventful one. It was largely occupied by his professional and literary activities and his home sheltered his many other interests. Part of it was an 'elaboratory', as he termed it, for his chemical

2 *Sir Thomas and Dame Dorothy Browne. An oil-painting attributed to Mrs Joan Carlile (1606?–1679); this portrait was probably painted shortly after their marriage in 1641 when Browne was thirty-six and his wife was twenty years of age.*

experiments and studies in natural history: it contained his notable collection of birds' eggs, maps and medals and housed his library of about 2000 volumes. He corresponded with leading intellectuals of his time in this country and abroad and was blessed with a happy marriage. Browne never moved from Norwich save to visit his county patients and friends or in pursuit of his interests in natural history and antiquarian matters in the East Anglian countryside.

Described by a friend as 'a man of modesty and kindness and one who was never idle', in appearance 'his complexion and hair was answerable to his name, his stature moderate [and] his modesty was visible in a natural habitual blush. . . . In his habit of clothing he had an aversion to all finery . . . he ever wore a cloke, or boots, when few others did.' Knighted by Charles II at the age of sixty-five years, Browne remained active to the last and died at his home after a week's illness on his seventy-seventh birthday – 'a remarkable Coincidence'.

Family

*'Generations passe while some trees stand, and old Families last not three Oaks' (**1**, 166).*

Browne's forebears were farmers at Upton, Cheshire; his father, also Thomas Browne, was a mercer in the City of London with two brothers, one a fellow mercer and the second a grocer who became Browne's guardian on his father's death in 1613. Browne's mother, Anne Garroway from Acton, Middlesex, had five children, Thomas and four daughters, three of whom married. By his own marriage to Dorothy Mileham (**2**) Browne had twelve children though only four survived their parents. The Milehams were an old Norfolk

3 *The Mileham memorial in the Church of St Andrew, North Burlingham. Originally in the Church of St Peter, North Burlingham, now a ruin, it was transferred to its present site in 1938. The memorial is dated 1615 when it was erected by Edward Mileham, father of Dame Dorothy Browne, in memory of his parents.*

family from North Burlingham (**3**) having connections by marriage with other Norfolk families. Dorothy Mileham's paternal grandmother married a Fountaine by her second marriage, her mother was a Hobart, her aunt married a Denny, a sister a Tenison and a half-sister another Tenison, brother of Thomas Tenison (**13**). Thus both through his marriage and also through those who became his friends and patients, Browne's writings often tell of the leading Norfolk families of his day. His domestic correspondence recounting his wife's culinary activities, his daughter Elizabeth reading to him in the evenings, the visits of their grandson and other family scenes reflect a singularly happy home life. The Reverend John Whitefoot who knew the Brownes throughout their married life wrote of Dame Dorothy as 'A Lady of such a Symetrical Proportion to her worthy Husband, both in the Graces of her Body and Mind, that they seemed to come together by a kind of Natural Magnetism.'

Edward (**4**), the Brownes' eldest son, became a physician of distinction in London and Thomas, the second son, died unmarried in his early twenties after a short career of bravery and promise as a lieutenant in the Royal Navy. There were three other sons, including twins, who died in infancy. Four of the Browne daughters married: the second, Anne, married the grandson by his second son of Viscount Fairfax of Emely, Ireland. A fifth daughter Mary died unmarried at the age of twenty-four years and two daughters died in infancy. Six of the Browne children are buried in the Church of St Peter Mancroft together with two of Anne Fairfax's children.

The Browne's eldest grandchild was 'Little Tomey', son of Edward, who spent long periods as a child with his grandparents in their Norwich home and is often referred to in Browne's letters to Edward and in charming postscripts to them by Dame Dorothy Browne who never appears to have acquired the art of spelling. 'Little Tomey' became a member of the medical profession and probably practised with his father. He married but left no surviving children and with his early death following a fall from a horse in 1710, the male line of Sir Thomas Browne became extinct. Nineteen grandchildren were born to Sir

Thomas and Dame Dorothy Browne and in the third generation their daughter Anne Fairfax's sixth child, Frances, married the fourth Lord Cardross and ninth Earl of Buchan. One of their grandchildren Thomas, born in 1750, became Lord High Chancellor and was created Lord Erskine of Restormel Castle, Cornwall. The members of these Buchan and Erskine families living at the present time are direct descendants of Sir Thomas Browne.

House and Garden

'Gardens were before Gardiners, and but some hours after the earth' (**1**, *179*).

Where Browne lived after his arrival at Norwich in 1636 is unknown. Between 1643 and 1649 he lived either in Upper King Street or Tombland and then took possession of a house in the Haymarket (**5**) where he lived and practised until his death thirty-two years later. Purchased from Alexander Anguish, Mayor of Norwich, its drawing-room indicates a

5 *Sir Thomas Browne's house in the Haymarket, demolished in 1842.*

sumptuously appointed abode (**6**). After Dame Dorothy Browne's death it passed to another physician Dr Roger Howman and then to his son Dr Edward Howman who in about 1739 presented what is now known as the Mancroft portrait of Sir Thomas Browne (**1**) to the Church of St Peter Mancroft. After Dr Edward Howman's retirement in 1745 the ground floor of the house was converted to a china and glass warehouse until 1842 when it was demolished and a savings bank built on the site (**7**). In its turn the bank was demolished in 1892 to make way for the trams (**9**) and the present rounded-off corner building at the junction of the Haymarket and Orford Place was built (**8**). On the opposite side of the Haymarket from Browne's house a group of buildings, including the White Horse Inn, occupied the centre of Hay Hill (**9**). These were demolished at the beginning of the present century and left an appropriate site for the statue of Browne, erected in 1905, which is sheltered from the north by the church where he is buried (**11**). If the bronze statue of Browne, depicting him in meditative posture, could raise its head this would be looking at the site of his house.

On a visit to Browne in 1671 John Evelyn described 'his whole house and garden being a paradise and cabinet of rarities, and that of the best collection, especially medals, books,

6 *The drawing-room of Browne's house in 1841, the year before the house was demolished. The carved oak overmantel, now in the collections of the Norfolk Museums Service, is the only part of the house to have survived. In its centre is a richly ornamented carving of the arms of King James I beneath which is the inscription 'Exurgat Deus dissipentur inimici' ('O God arise and scatter our enemies'). On each side of the centrepiece is a boss of yellow onyx.*

7 *Norwich Savings Bank, 1843, built on the site of Browne's house, and demolished in 1892.*

8 *This plaque on the wall of 5 Orford Place was erected in 1969 and replaced an earlier commemorative metal plate.*

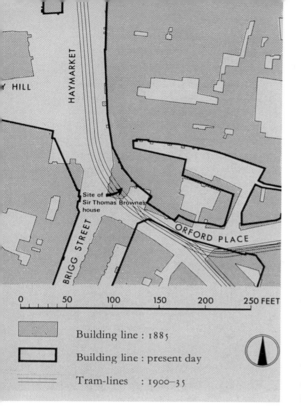

9 *Map to show the site of Browne's house. The speckled areas denote the buildings of 1885 and the black line the present-day building line. The tramlines along the Haymarket and Orford Place were laid at the end of the nineteenth century and removed in 1935.*

Building line : 1885

Building line : present day

Tram-lines : 1900–35

10 *Sir Thomas Browne's Garden House, demolished in 1961, is traditionally believed to have stood in or adjacent to the garden of Browne's residence. At its demolition a fine plaster ceiling and a door were preserved. The ceiling, owned and stored by Norwich City Council, awaits a suitable house in which to install it. The door is preserved in the Strangers' Hall Museum where it hangs in a doorway between the Exhibition Room and a landing above stairs to the Sotherton Room. In Browne's day the Strangers' Hall was the residence of Sir Joseph Paine, a wealthy hosier, Mayor of Norwich in 1660 and, as Browne wrote, 'Collonell [of] . . . our Regiment of the Citty' in the Norfolk militia (4, 9, 14).*

plants, and natural things'. Among Browne's surviving writings is a list of the seeds he had purchased from the Botanical Garden at Oxford, of those that came up and in which beds they were sown. Additional observations in another hand, probably that of his son Dr Edward Browne, add further details as to where the seeds were sown 'towards the stable, next the kitchin, next the south wall . . . all under the long walk by the hors radish els' (3, 397–400). The exact boundaries of Browne's garden where Evelyn walked with him are not known but the garden extended north from Browne's residence and included part of the site now occupied by Littlewoods' store. When this store was built in the 1960s an Elizabethan house, long known as Sir Thomas Browne's Garden House, was demolished to make way for it (10).

11 *The unveiling of Browne's statue on Hay Hill by Lord Avebury (formerly Sir John Lubbock) in 1905 at the tercentenary of Browne's birth. When alterations, including the erection of a fountain, were made to Hay Hill in 1972, Browne's statue was moved. Its original site east of the fountain is marked by brickwork in the pattern of a quincunx.*

12 *The Church of St Peter Mancroft and the Market Place, Norwich, in the eighteenth century.*

Church of
St Peter Mancroft

'At my devotion I love to use the civility of my knee, my hat, and hands. . . . At the sight of a Crosse or Crucifix I can dispence with my hat, but scarce with the thought and memory of my Saviour' (1, 12–13).

The Church of St Peter Mancroft (**12**), built between 1430 and 1455 in the Perpendicular style, dominates the south side of Norwich Market Place. It has been justly claimed to have 'few rivals among the parish churches of England for its beauty, its unity and its unique position in city life'. Browne is its most famous parishioner, he worshipped there and with his wife and eight descendants he is buried there. It has been said of the church's altar that 'it linked his practice to his library and both of these to God'.

The main structure of the church is little changed from Browne's day but when he moved to the parish in 1650 the church would have lacked its beauty and serenity of today. In 1643 Cromwell's troops had destroyed its vestments, furnishings and ornaments and in 1644 its pictures; Christmas services were banned from 1645. All its windows were covered with sailcloth for in 1648 a store of gunpowder on the site of the present Bethel Hospital was set afire during rioting between Royalists and Puritans. The explosion killed 100 people and blew in the windows of the Church of St Peter Mancroft. Much glass by the famous fifteenth-century Norwich glassmakers was lost but during repair work over four years sufficient remained to reglaze the church's great east window though the windows were to suffer further damage in a 'great tempest of wynde' in 1661. There were no pews and only a few backless benches, introduced in the sixteenth century, one of which stands today in St Anne's Chapel. Other surviving items of church furnishings from Browne's time are the octagonal tester of the pulpit 'of the time of Charles I', returned to the church in 1893 and now serving as a table-top in the sacristy, where there is additionally an elaborately inlaid writing-desk dating from the reign of Charles II. The church's fine pieces of sixteenth- and

13 *Thomas Tenison (1636–1715), of Norfolk clerical forbears and a scholar of Norwich School (King Edward VI), was Upper Minister (Vicar) of the Church of St Peter Mancroft from 1674 to 1676 and later Vicar of St Martin-in-the-Fields, Bishop of Lincoln and Archbishop of Canterbury. He edited the first edition of Browne's* Miscellany Tracts *in 1683. His uncle the Reverend Philip Tenison, Archdeacon of Norfolk and buried in the chancel of Bawburgh Church in 1660, married Anne, Dame Dorothy Browne's sister, and his brother William married Dame Dorothy's half-sister Margaret.*

seventeenth-century plate include the famous Gleane Cup presented in 1633 by Sir Peter Gleane, Mayor of Norwich and one of Browne's circle of friends. The church's minister at the time of Browne taking up residence in the parish was John Carter, a red-hot Puritan, and it is doubtful if Browne then worshipped at the church or if so, from the records available, not on a regular basis.

In 1660 the bells of the Church of St Peter Mancroft rang out to celebrate the Restoration, the order of the Church of England returned to its cathedrals and parish churches and Browne came regularly to worship at the Church of St Peter Mancroft for, as the Reverend John

Whitefoot has recorded, he 'attended the publick service very constantly . . . and never missed the sacrament in his parish, if he were in town'. During Charles II's reign the first pews were installed in the church, of oak panels painted black, and other works of restoration were carried out. Browne was influential in obtaining the services of his wife's kinsman the Reverend Thomas Tenison (**13**) as Upper Minister, or Vicar, of the Church, from 1674 to 1676 and of his friend the Reverend John Jeffrey, later Archdeacon of Norwich, in 1678. With Browne's daughter Elizabeth Lyttleton, Jeffrey, an ardent admirer of Browne, edited Browne's *Christian Morals* in 1716. He probably presided over Browne's interment and is himself buried in the sanctuary near the Browne vault.

Browne wrote that 'at my death I meane to take a totall adieu of the world, not caring for a Monument, History, or Epitaph, not so much as the bare memory of my name to be found any where but in the universall Register of God' (**1**, 51). But the first of many to ignore this passage was his wife who 'caused to be erected' the memorial to Browne on the south wall of the sanctuary above his vault (**14**) and it is the third oldest memorial in the church. After her own death three years later, their son Edward wrote the epitaph for her memorial erected on the wall opposite (**15**). There are no memorials to the Brownes' children and grandchildren buried in the church except to their daughter Mary who died in 1676. Surmounted by the Browne coat of arms her inscription occupies the central five lines of a stone lying below the altar steps and half covered by the south choir stalls.

14 *Sir Thomas Browne's memorial of black and white marble in the Church of St Peter Mancroft. In the epitaph Browne is described as* 'per orbem Notissimus Vir Pientissimus, Integerrimus, Doctissimus' – 'a man very pious, whole, learned and famed throughout the world'.

Norwich Cathedral

*'This Church for its spire may compare in a manner with any in England . . . butt lower then that of Salisbury' (**3**, 142–3).*

Browne had close associations with Norwich Cathedral. A number of its bishops, deans and prebendaries were his patients – and friends – and their names recur in his letters where Browne often records his attendance, and that of his family, at divine services in the Cathedral, which he refers to as 'Christ Church' or 'Xt Church'. In 1680, as almost his last piece of writing, Browne wrote *Repertorium, or Some Account of the Tombs and Monuments in the Cathedral Church of Norwich. Repertorium* had as its object a record of all the monuments in the Cathedral many of which had been destroyed or damaged in the Puritan sacking of the Cathedral in 1643. His account was based on some notes made twenty years previously with the help of John Wright, one of the clerks, and John Sandlin, a member of the choir who had

16 *An engraving of Norwich Cathedral illustrating Browne's* Repertorium.

been a chorister in the reign of Queen Elizabeth I; Sandlin was also the 'Keeper of the Ferry' and what is now known as Pull's Ferry, after John Pull the ferryman from 1786 to 1841, was previously known as Sandlin's Ferry for 150 years. Browne rewrote *Repertorium* in 1680 and two copies in his own hand are preserved in the Norfolk Record Office. It was first published in his *Posthumous Works* of 1712, with a number of illustrations among which was the adjacent engraving of the Cathedral (**16**). *Repertorium* is not a literary work but is a valuable record of the Cathedral memorials in the seventeenth century.

15 *The memorial to Dame (Lady) Dorothy Browne in the Church of St Peter Mancroft. Her arms are those of Browne of Upton, Cheshire impaled with those of Mileham of Burlingham, Norfolk.*

17 *The tomb of the Reverend Miles Spencer, Chancellor of Norwich Cathedral from 1537 to 1575, in the eighth bay from east to west of the south aisle, Norwich Cathedral. Chancellor Spencer lived to the age of ninety years and was the last Dean of the Collegiate Church of St Mary in the Fields, that stood on the site of the garden in front of the Assembly House. On the Chancellor's tomb Browne paid the rent for his meadow at Michaelmas.*

18 *Norwich in the early eighteenth century. From the River Wensum in the foreground a canal passes under a monastic watergate (Pull's Ferry) and the second meadow on the left (south) of the canal from its junction with the Wensum has the abuttals described for Browne's Meadow. The canal was filled in about 1780.*

Browne's Meadow

'In a meddow I use in this citty, besett about with sallowes, I have observed there to growe upon their bare heads builders, corants, gooseberries, cynocrambe, Rasberries, barberries, bittersweet, elder, hawthorne' (3, 378).

The records of the Dean and Chapter of Norwich Cathedral show that from 1669 they granted to Browne the lease of a 'little meadowe in the precinct . . . during his naturell life'. The site of the meadow is shown in an engraving of Norwich of the early eighteenth century (**18**) and though it has been suggested that Browne may have used it to graze his horses, from the quotation cited he appears to have used it as an extension to his garden in the Haymarket. The Dean and Chapter Ledger Books record that for the lease of the meadow Browne paid 'the sume of ten shillings of lawful money of England at the Feast of Saint Michael the Archangell . . . upon the tombe commonly called Doctor Spencer's tombe' (**17**). In his

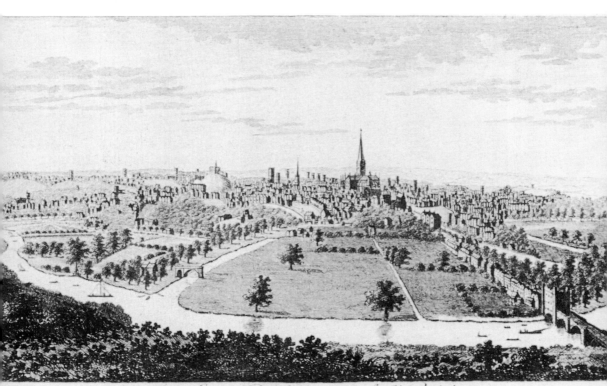

The South East View of the City of Norwich.

Repertorium Browne described this tomb as 'covered with a kind of Touchstone . . . [that] was entire, butt now broken, splitt and depressed by blowes: more speciall notice being taken of this stone, because men used to trie their money upon it, and because the chapter demanded their Rents at this tomb' (**3, 123**).

In later years houses were built on part of the meadow's site and the remainder became the vegetable garden for the Dean of Norwich, then allotments for residents in The Close. During the 1970s these were converted to a car park that extends from the back of the houses on the north side of Recorder Road to Ferry Lane between Nos. 20 and 21 The Close. A plaque erected in 1982 marks the site.

19 *Simon Wilkin (1790–1862), son of a miller at Costessey, Norwich, had a varied career in Norwich, including that of a publisher, before moving to London. In 1835–36 he edited after twelve years of 'scholarship and painstaking care' a four-volume edition of Browne's works, his correspondence and much original material gleaned from manuscript sources.*

20 *Engraved title-page from the first unauthorised edition of* Religio Medici *(1642).*

Wilkin Collection and Browne's Works

Browne *'wrote because he loved to write; he enjoyed using words as a painter enjoys using paint. But, in the art of writing, the medium is inseparable from the meaning; Browne used words to convey meaning. . . . Everything he writes is saturated in personality; his curiosity, his sense of wonder, his amusement, his faith in the harmonious order of the universe are all mirrored in the way he uses the language. He may use it clumsily or superbly well, but he cannot use it commonly'* – Mrs Joan Bennett *(1962).*

In Norwich Central Library is housed one of five special collections of Browne's works; the other four are in London, Glasgow, Montreal and Los Angeles, that in London being moved to Cambridge after mid 1982. It is the collection assembled by Simon Wilkin (**19**) and presented to the City of Norwich by his daughter-in-law, Mrs Martin Hood Wilkin, on the day of the tercentenary of Browne's birth, 19 October 1905. Comprising sixty volumes and manuscripts the Wilkin Collection is divided between Norwich Central Library and the Norfolk Record Office, both housed in the same building. Among its treasures are two of the eight known manuscript copies of *Religio*

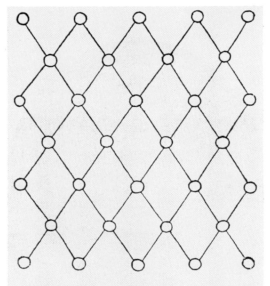

Quid Quincunce speciosius, qui, in quam cunqꝫ partem spectaueris, rectus est. Quintilian: //

21 'Quid quincunce: *What is more handsome than the quincunx, which, in whatsoever direction you look, is straight? Quintilian*' from Browne's The Garden of Cyrus or The Quincunciall . . . *(1658)*.

22 'En sum: *See I am a burden which is lifted by five fingers*', from Browne's Hydriotaphia or Urne-Burial *(1658)*.

En sum quod digitis Quinque levatur onus properi.

Medici, not as once claimed in Browne's own hand, copies of the first unauthorised 1642, (**20**) and authorised, 1643, editions of *Religio Medici* and John Evelyn's copy of the first edition of *Miscellany Tracts*, 1683, with Evelyn's signature, motto and annotations.

Browne's *Religio Medici*, the exploration of his own religion, was his first and most famous work and has been published in eight languages and over a hundred editions. The second was his longest, *Pseudodoxia Epidemica: or, Enquiries into Very many received Tenents, And commonly presumed Truths*, also known as *Vulgar Errors*; first published in 1646 and six times revised, this large volume was designed to combat the popularity of a variety of erroneous beliefs and displays Browne's erudition, his depth of reading and his own thought, observation and experiment. His next work to be written, though not published until after his death, was *A Letter to a Friend, Upon occasion of the Death of his Intimate Friend*, a literary fantasy based on the clinical history of a patient with pulmonary tuberculosis whom Browne attended.

In 1658 Browne published in one volume *Hydriotaphia or Urne-Burial* and *The Garden of Cyrus* (**21**) that have been termed 'the luxuriant products of his middle age'. *Urne-Burial* (**22**) is the leisurely excursion of a scholarly mind into the burial customs of past nations and of its concluding chapter the claim has been made that 'for richness of imagery and majestic pomp of diction [it] can hardly be paralleled in the English language'. Browne's three remaining volumes – *Miscellany Tracts, Posthumous Works* and *Christian Morals* – were all published after his death and he also left a large number of manuscript notes and letters to friends and relatives. These manuscripts and letters were first assembled and published, together with Browne's works and a memoir on Browne's life based on his own researches, by Simon Wilkin in 1835–36. The task took Wilkin twelve years to complete but as Sir Geoffrey Keynes has written, 'the foundation of the work.of all later editions was laid by him . . . and there is little to add to Wilkin's biographical researches.'

In addition to its manuscripts from the Wilkin Collection, the Norfolk Record Office possesses two holograph manuscripts of *Repertorium*, Browne's will (**23**) and a list of fourteen volumes of Browne's works, kept in Norwich Central Library, that were presented by the daughter of Dr W. A. Greenhill to the City of Norwich, again on 19 October 1905. A physician and classicist who practised at Oxford and Hastings, Greenhill's edition of Browne's *Religio Medici*, published for Macmillan's Golden Treasury Series in 1881, was for long the most authoritative text and was many times reprinted. Norwich Central Library also contains the writings on Browne by Charles Williams, a Norwich surgeon of whom Sir William Osler self-effacingly said in 1905 that 'he was more familiar than any one living with the history of Browne', and in the library of the Art Department of Norwich Castle Museum there are three volumes of the 'Williams Bequest 1907' comprising a unique collection of prints, engravings and photographs relating to the life of Browne that Williams assembled.

23 *Part of Browne's original will, dated 1679, written in his own hand and proved in the Consistory Court of Norwich.*

24 *Engraved portrait by Robert White of Browne, reproduced with* Collected Works *(1686).*

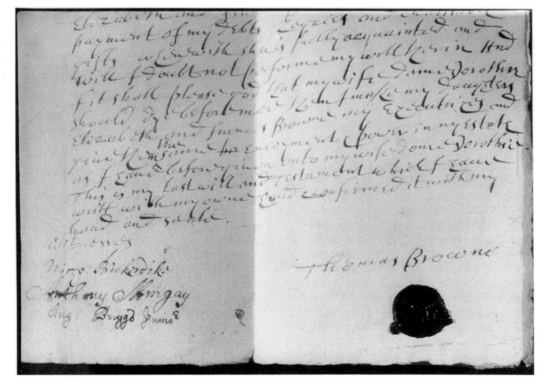

A volume with an especial interest is one presented by Browne to the Norwich City Library formed in 1608 and recorded in its lists of donations as 'Opera Sua, viz. Religio Medici, Vulgar Errors, &c.'; this well-preserved volume contains autograph corrections to its texts by Browne. In 1666 he also gave to the library eight volumes of Justus Lipsius' Works (Antwerp, 1606–17) described in the library's Vellum Book of gifts as donated by 'Thomas Browne, Med: Professor.' (**37**)

Physician

*'Some consideration we hope from the course of our Profession, which though it leadeth us into many truths that pass undiscerned by others, yet doth it disturb their Communications, and much interrupt the office of our Pens in their well intended Transmissions.... This work ... being composed by snatches of time, as medical vacations, and the fruitless importunity of Uroscopy would permit us . . . is not to be performed upon one legg; and should smel of oyl, if duly and deservedly handled' (**2**, **4**).*

As Browne explained in the foregoing lines from the preface to his *Vulgar Errors* his literary work took second place to his professional duties. He had an active life as the leading East Anglian physician of his day often being absent from home over several days visiting his county patients by coach or on horseback. In his letters and other writings there are accounts of his visits to the homes of distinguished Norfolk families, whether Royalist like the Pastons or Puritan like the Hobarts, and others are cited in Browne's *Norfolk*. He also attended the poor for nothing or by payment from the parish rate. Thus he visited 'a poore woeman . . . [who] dwells in one of the towers of the [Norwich city] wall' (**4**, 168) and 'David Brand's chylde of St George Colegate [suffering from] . . . sores'. Browne described epidemics of plague and smallpox in Norwich, malaria, so common in East Anglia during his day, and diseases such as gout and bladder stone. Apart from quinine and opium there were no effective drugs available and most of his prescribing was with the common

herbal polypharmacy of the time. A number of these prescriptions survive in the Household Book kept by the ladies of Gunton Park where Browne attended the Harbord family. The book was kept at the house for 300 years and at the sale of its contents in 1980 was given to the Church of St Peter Mancroft.

Browne made no scientific contributions to medicine but he read all the newly published medical works of his time and of the greatest medical advance of his time, Harvey's discovery of the circulation of the blood, wrote that 'I prefer [it] to that of Columbus' (**4**, 255). His only original observation was the description of adipocere in a body found in a Norfolk churchyard (**1**, 156) but he did engage in experiments on embryology and coagulation, though they largely failed. Browne lived in a century that witnessed a great explosion in science and knowledge and while in his writings he often appeared more medieval than modern Browne realised that the age in which he lived had made the intellectual turn.

His *métier* was that of the humanist physician, displaying a great understanding of his patients with kindliness and tolerance and with the faculty of making them feel better for having seen him. His famous disciple and fellow physician and humanist, Sir William Osler, who lived 250 years later, said to a group of medical students that the three lessons they could learn from Browne's life were those of 'mastery of self, conscientious devotion to duty [and] deep interest in human beings'. As judged by the standards and state of knowledge of his time and by his impact on the people of Norfolk, Browne can be regarded as a good physician and this judgement was supported by the action of the Fellows of the Royal College of Physicians of London in electing him to an Honorary Fellowship of the College in 1664 (**25**), the first and only Norfolk physician to achieve this honour.

25 *Browne's Diploma of Honorary Fellowship of the Royal College of Physicians of London, 1664, reproduced in* Posthumous Works *(1712). In the citation he is described as 'virtute et literis ornatissimum Virum' – 'a man eminently endowed with virtue and literature'.*

Antiquary and Natural Historian

'Time which antiquates Antiquities, and hath an art to make dust of all things, hath yet spared these minor Monuments' (1, 164).

'All things are artificiall, for Nature is the Art of God' (1, 26).

Browne was attracted by anything of antiquity. Hence his interest in medals, in the urns found at Great Walsingham and Brampton and a fossil bone at Winterton. His reputation in this field extended beyond Norfolk. He corresponded with Sir William Dugdale, the most celebrated antiquary of his day and Garter King-of-Arms. Dugdale was engaged in writing a book, *The History of Imbarking and Drayning of divers Fenns and Marshes*, published in 1662; in this he acknowledged the 'considerable assistance' of Browne who provided him with information on the East Anglian fens. Browne also corresponded with two other seventeenth-century antiquaries, William Lilly and Elias Ashmole, whose gifts to Oxford University formed the basis of its Ashmolean Museum.

Browne was an accomplished naturalist and his notes on the birds, fishes and plants of Norfolk are of such interest that in 1902 they were published as a separate volume. He was Norfolk's first scientific ornithologist; he made original observations on bitterns (26), noted migratory habits of birds long before they were generally appreciated and is thought to have been the first to make a careful study and collection of birds' eggs. From fishermen he collected specimens of marine life and among his many observations on plants are the first records of Sea Holly (*Eryngium maritimum*) that he observed on Great Yarmouth sands and Sweet Flag (*Acorus calamus*) (27). In the field of natural history he again achieved a national reputation and corresponded with Dr Christopher Merrett, Fellow and Librarian of the Royal College of Physicians of London, who in 1666 published a book on the natural history of Great Britain. Browne was also in touch with John Ray, a greater naturalist than Merrett, lending him 'many draughts of birds in colours' for his volumes on ornithology; in their prefaces Ray acknowledged his indebtedness to 'the deservedly famous Sir Thomas Browne, Professor of Physic in the City of Norwich' (4, 216). As further illustrations of Browne's interest in natural history some random examples are quoted in Browne's Norfolk.

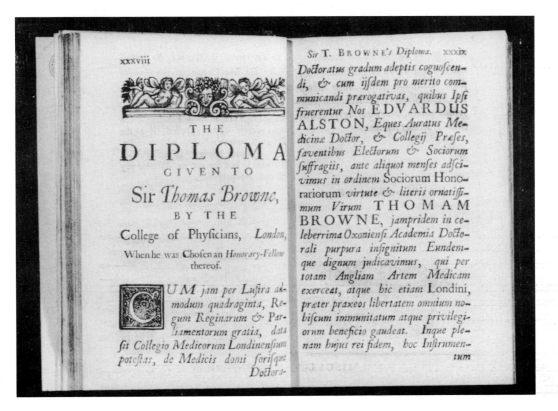

26 *Bittern,* Botaurus stellaris, *a resident in Broadland and winter visitor to reedbeds in other parts of the county. Browne kept a bittern in the yard of his house for two years; he observed that contrary to the then popular belief bitterns did not produce their peculiar booming by putting their bills into hollow reeds or into mud and water.*

27 Acorus calamus, *Sweet Flag. First described by Browne in 1643: 'This elegant plant groweth very* plentifully and beareth its Julus *yearly by the bankes of Norwich river, chiefly about Claxton and Surlingham & also between Norwich and Hellsden bridge, so that I have known Heigham Church in the suburbes of Norwich strowed all over with it' (4, 344). Heigham Church (St Bartholomew's) was completely destroyed by bombs, except for its tower, in the Second World War. Acorus calamus today is rare in the west but frequent in east Norfolk; it grows in the margins of ponds and riversides.*

Knighthood

'Our gratious Soveraygne now Reygning King Charles the second [visited Norwich], of which I had particular reason to take notice. (3, 143).

In 1671 Charles II with his Queen Catherine of Braganza, a number of persons about his Court and many attendants, visited Norwich. They stayed with Lord Henry Howard, later sixth Duke of Norfolk, at his Palace (**28**) where an account records that 'the great tennis court was turned into a kitchen, the bowling alley was converted into five separate dining rooms . . . a splendid banquet was set before hundreds of people and the Dukes and grandees of the court, and their countless attendants all slept . . . beneath the Palace roof.' The King's programme included a service in the Cathedral, a visit to the Bishop's Palace, and a review of the local trained bands from the leads of the Guildhall when a great crowd of citizens in the Market Place acclaimed him. He was then conducted to a civic banquet in St Andrew's Hall (**29**) where he proposed to knight the Mayor, Thomas Thacker. The Mayor modestly declined the honour and in the words of Matthew Stephenson, a Norfolk poet of the day:

'Then the King knighted the so famous Browne
Whose worth and learning to the world are known.'

28 *Duke's Palace, Norwich, its bowling-alley in the early nineteenth century from the River Wensum. The bowling-alley survived the demolition of the Palace in 1711 after the eighth Duke of Norfolk had left Norwich in a fit of pique following a quarrel with the Mayor of Norwich. It was then leased by the Dukes of Norfolk to the Court of Guardians as a workhouse and part of the building survived into the present century. Dr Edward Browne described the banquets and dances he attended at the Palace in the 1660s and Charles II with his Court stayed there in 1671.*

The main Palace building stood at the junction of the present-day Duke Street with Charing Cross and St Andrew's Street; its gardens and 'left-wing', of which the ducal bowling-alley was part, extended along the east side of Duke Street to the River Wensum.

29 *The Norwich Blackfriars in the late seventeenth century; the tower fell in 1712. This former Church of the Dominicans (Black Friars) was adopted as a municipal building at the Reformation. During the seventeenth century the chancel (Blackfriars Hall) was still used for services; now in secular use the civic portraits hanging on its walls depict a number of Browne's seventeenth-century contemporaries. The nave (New Hall, St Andrew's Hall) was converted after the Reformation into an assembly hall and used, as it still is, for a wide variety of functions. In this hall the Mayor of Norwich in 1671 held a banquet for Charles II when Browne was knighted.*

The South Prospect of
Black-friers Church in
Norwich.

Skull

'To be gnaw'd out of our graves . . . [is a] Tragicall abomination, escaped in burning Burials' (1, 155).

'But who knows the fate of his bones, or how often he is to be buried?' (1, 131).

Below Browne's memorial in the sanctuary of the Church of St Peter Mancroft a tablet records the death in 1840 of Mary Bowman, wife of the then incumbent. During the digging of her grave Browne's coffin was accidentally broken by workmen. The skull and coffin-plate were abstracted by Robert Fitch, who planned to return them but when he came to do so the grave was refilled and sealed. Fitch, a chemist and druggist and a keen antiquary, was elected Churchwarden of St Peter Mancroft five years later and his name survives in the church below a light to his

memory in the altar window of St Anne's Chapel. The fate of the skull over the next five years is unknown but in 1845 it was presented to the Museum of the Norfolk and Norwich Hospital by Dr Edward Lubbock, a hospital physician. The coffin-plate (30), broken in two pieces, remained in a drawer of Fitch's desk where it was found at his death in 1895 and returned to the Church of St Peter Mancroft. Only one half now survives and is kept in the sacristy.

In the Museum of the Norfolk and Norwich Hospital Browne's skull was kept under a glass bell-jar until 1901 when Dr William Osler, later Sir William Osler, Regius Professor of Medicine at Oxford University and a lifelong admirer of Browne, presented a glass casket to contain it (31). Then in 1922 after many years of pressure by the Church of St Peter Mancroft for the return of the skull, the hospital authorities returned it to the church after first arranging for its examination at the Royal College of

30 Browne's coffin-plate, an impression taken from the original coffin-plate and mounted on the pedestal of Osler's casket (**31**). The original coffin-plate was broken in two and only one half survives. The inscription was composed by Dr Edward Browne and its last lines read 'hoc Loculo indormiens, Corporis Spagyrici pulvere plumbum in aurum Convertit' – 'sleeping in this coffin, by the dust of his alchemic body, he converts the lead into gold'.

31 Osler's casket to house Browne's skull, in the Sir Thomas Browne Library, Norfolk and Norwich Hospital. Since the skull's reinterral in 1922 the casket has contained a cast of Browne's skull. The front plate on the base of the casket records that Osler donated the casket to the Norfolk and Norwich Hospital in 1901; the inscriptions on the three other plates on each side of the skull are quotations selected by Osler from Religio Medici.

Surgeons of England where it was confirmed to be Browne's skull. The skull was taken for this examination in London by special messenger in a box that is still kept in the sacristy of St Peter Mancroft. During its years of absence from a grave five casts were made of the skull. One replaced the original skull in Osler's casket, a second is in the Church of St Peter Mancroft and a third in Norwich Castle Museum; the two others are in London. After the return of Browne's skull from London it was reinterred at a special service at the Church of St Peter Mancroft conducted by its then Vicar, the Reverend Canon F. J. Meyrick, who had played a prominent role in obtaining the return of the skull. Its age was recorded in the burial register as '317 years' and the site of its reinterral below Browne's memorial is marked on a sanctuary step by the following inscription composed by the Right Reverend Bertram Pollock, Bishop of Norwich from 1910 to 1942:

T   B

O CAPUT AUGUSTUM PETRO
CUSTODE SEPULCHRI
SIT TIBI PAX NOMEN VIVAT IN URBE
VALE
MDCCCC   XXII

Envoi

Throughout his Norwich life Browne lived up to his own exacting precept to 'tread softly and circumspectly in this funambulatory Track and narrow Path of Goodness' (1, 243). In this memoir it has been possible to depict something of such personal qualities and the beauty of his prose. The reader may be inspired to learn more through his own study of Browne's life and works.

'O noble head lie safe in Peter's keeping,
May peace be with thee and thy name,
Be ever loved in this thy city. Farewell.'

Browne's Norfolk

'Let any stranger find mee out so pleasant a county, such good way, large heath, three such places as Norwich, Yar. and Lin. in any county of England, and I'll bee once again a vagabond to visit them.'

From a *Journal of a Tour of Derbyshire* (1662) by Sir Thomas Browne's sons, Edward and Thomas.

Map of Browne's Norfolk – see inside front cover.

Ashwellthorpe

The Royalist Thomas Knyvett of Ashwellthorpe wrote to his wife in 1644 about the illness of their elder daughter 'meddle no further with Physsick with out an Apparant necessety and the Advise of Dr Browne.'

Blickling

Browne described a thunderstorm in 1665 when a 'fire ball went of in Sr John Hobarts gallerie at Blickling: hee was so neere that his arme & thigh were nummed above an hower after' (**3**, 240).

Brampton

In 1667 Browne wrote a short antiquary's piece *Concerning some urnes found in Brampton feild in Norfolk*. These Roman urns were found 'in a large arable feild lying between Buxton and Brampton . . . not much more than a furlong from Oxned Park . . . upon notice given unto mee I went unto the place myself' (**1**, 233). Current excavations and fieldwork, commenced in 1965, have revealed evidence of an important Romano-British settlement at Brampton.

Bungay, Suffolk

In a thunderstorm in 1665 'a woeman & horse were killed neere Bungay; her hatt so shivered that no peece remained bigger than a groat, whereof I had some peeces sent unto mee' (**3**, 240).

Shire Hall & Court House, Bury St Edmunds.

Rock & Co London. No 1854.   June 1st 1851.

32 *Shire Hall and Court House, Bury St Edmunds in 1851. The Assize Court, where Browne gave evidence at a trial of two women accused of sorcery in 1664, was held in the then Grand Jury House, renamed the Shire Hall when colonnades were added in the nineteenth century (on the left). In 1904, together with the* adjacent Magpie Inn, the Shire Hall was demolished to make way for the present West Suffolk Shire Hall and Court Rooms. The Manor House, Honey Hill, on the right of the engraving, still stands; once the Court House it now houses the Justices' Clerk's Office for the local Magistrates' Courts.

Bury St Edmunds, Suffolk
In 1664 a trial was held at the Assize Court (**32**) before Sir Matthew Hale, Lord Chief Baron of the Exchequer, of two women accused of sorcery. Browne, a believer in witchcraft, was summoned to give testimony. The women were found guilty and hanged.

Chediston (Cheston), Suffolk
Browne's *A Letter to a Friend, Upon occasion of the Death of his Intimate Friend*, was based on the clinical history of a patient whom Browne attended for his terminal pulmonary tuberculosis. Thirty years ago the 'intimate friend' was identified by Professor F. L. Huntley as Robert Loveday, a man of letters of the Loveday family of Chediston, Suffolk and the 'friend' as his neighbour Sir John Pettus,

owner of Chediston Hall. Only the walls of the old hall's garden remain and a contemporary hall has been built on the site of the old one.

Claxton
In 1665 Browne wrote to his son Edward that 'the sicknesse [the plague] wch God so long withheld from us is now in Norwich. I intend to send your sisters to Claxton, & if it encreaseth to remove 3 or 4 miles of, where I may bee serviceable upon occasion to my freinds in other diseases' (**4**, 28). The plague did increase and over 2000 Norwich citizens died from it during 1665–66.

Cromer
In 1665 during the Second Dutch War Browne wrote that 'wee heare also that a caper of

twentie gunnes was taken not farre from Cromer last Saturday by a frigat after 2 howers fight' (**4**, 28).

Crostwight (Crostwick)

In the seventeenth century the old Norfolk family of Le Gros lived at Crostwight Hall. Sir Charles Le Gros was one of Browne's friends who persuaded him to settle in Norwich and to his son Thomas, who shared his antiquarian interests, Browne dedicated his *Hydriotaphia or Urne-Burial*. In the chancel of Crostwight Church is a memorial to one of Sir Charles Le Gros's granddaughters and near by are the sixteenth-century ruins of Crostwight Hall amid a group of farm buildings. Both stand three miles from the North Sea, or as Browne wrote in his dedication to Thomas Le Gros, 'but few miles of known Earth between your self and the Pole' (**1**, 131).

Deopham (Depeham)

'An extraordinarie large & stately tilia, Linden or Lime tree there groweth at Depeham . . . the first motive I had to viewe it was not so much the largenesse of the tree as the generall opinion that no man could ever name it; butt I found it to bee a tilia faemina . . . [and] to distinguish it from others in the country I called it tilia colossea Depehamensis' (**4**, 280). The tree was blown down during a gale in 1713.

East Raynham (Raynham)

Sir Roger Townshend started in 1619 the building of Raynham Hall that excelled in size and architectural refinement both Blickling and Oxnead. Browne described it as the 'noblest pyle among us' (**1**, 131). Sir Roger died two years before Browne moved to Norwich and during his lifetime Raynham Hall was occupied by Sir Horatio Townshend, first Viscount Townshend and Lord-Lieutenant of Norfolk, described by Browne as a 'true Gentleman and my honored Friend' (**1**, 131). A staunch Royalist he was visited by Charles II in 1671.

Felbrigg (Felbrigge)

The stately south front of Felbrigg Hall was built in 1620 and a western wing added in 1686 (**33**). Here Browne attended Thomas Windham (*c.* 1585–1654) in his last illness and later his son John Windham (1622–65). On the latter occasion the Steward's Account Books record payment to Dr Browne of thirty shillings for his fees. The last owner of the house, R. W. Ketton-Cremer, a distinguished biographer, Norfolk historian and devotee of Browne, left the house to the National Trust on his death in 1969.

33 *Felbrigg Hall, where Browne attended two members of the Windham family.*

Gillingham

Browne dedicated *The Garden of Cyrus* to Nicholas Bacon (1623–66) of Gillingham where 'you have wisely ordered your vegetable delights, beyond the reach of exception' (**1**, 176). Browne had known Nicholas Bacon before he moved to Norwich and they shared scholarly and literary interests. Created a baronet by Charles II in 1661, Nicholas Bacon was grandson by his fourth son of that Sir Nicholas Bacon who was created the premier baronet of England in 1611 by James I. The premier baronetcy was held in the seventeenth century by a kinsman Sir Edmund Bacon whose descendant of the same christian name holds the title today. As Browne wrote, his friend was a member of 'a flourishing branch of that Noble Family, unto which we owe so much observance' (**1**, 177). Sir Nicholas's baronetcy passed in succession to two sons but neither of them had heirs and the title became extinct. Gillingham Hall, a Jacobean house of red brick plastered yellow, still stands and has a vegetable garden. There is a marble alabaster memorial to Sir Nicholas Bacon in the Norman Parish Church of St Mary, Gillingham.

Gorleston (Golston)

'I have founde it [*Urtica romana*] to grow wild at Golston by Yarmouth, & transplanted it to other places' (**4**, 344). Now known as *Urtica pilulifera* this plant gained its synonym of 'Roman Nettle' from the suggestion that Julius Caesar's invading soldiers used it 'to rubbe and chafe their limbs'.

Great Melton

During the Norwich outbreak of the plague in 1665–66 Browne appears to have sent his daughters to Claxton (q.v.) and himself moved to Great Melton. From Great Melton he wrote on 31 August 1666 to John Hobart 'at his howse in St Giles parish', Norwich, 'extremely troubled to heare that some have had the sicknesse [plague] in your howse'. Browne gave advice on 'possets' to drink and how to 'fume' (fumigate) the rooms of the house 'in order to prevention' (**4**, 383–4). John Hobart was a kinsman of Sir John Hobart of Blickling.

Great Walsingham (Old Walsingham)

When in 1658 'in a Field of Old Walsingham, not many moneths past, were digged up between fourty and fifty Urnes' (**1**, 140), Browne was inspired to write his *Hydriotaphia* or *Urne-Burial*. The site of this urn cemetery in Great Walsingham is not known and Browne was wrong in identifying the 'urnes' (**22**) as Roman for they were Saxon but this error he shared with his antiquarian successors for two centuries. One urn in the Ashmolean Museum, Oxford and two urns in the British Museum, London are claimed to be from this Great Walsingham cemetery.

Great Yarmouth (Yarmouth)

'Of Herring incredible shoales passe by this coast about 7tember untill towards the end of October. . . . Unto this fishing boats resort . . . wh. bring in herrings into Yarmouth. Such store sometimes is taken in a day that. . . , that is, above an herring for every man in England' (**3**, 431). Browne also described a number of visits by him to Great Yarmouth.

Gunton

In 1676 John Harbord, younger son of the Surveyor-General to Charles I and Charles II, purchased the Gunton estate and his collateral heirs, of whom one became the first Baronet in 1745 and another was created the first Lord Suffield in 1786, lived at Gunton Park until recent years. Here, in the last decade of his life, Browne attended the Harbord family; prescriptions by him were recorded in the Gunton Household Book and a contemporary portrait of him (**34**) hung in the house. On the sale of the contents of the house in 1980 the Trustees of the Gunton Park estate presented the Household Book and portrait to the Church of St Peter Mancroft, Norwich.

Hethersett (Hetherset)

Browne wrote to his son Edward in 1676, 'Mrs Hombarston hath been so ill that I was fayne to visit her at Hetherset, and the neibours were all afrayd shee would have dyed' (**4**, 64).

Horsham St Faith (St Fayth)

'This day [6 October 1679] beginneth St Fayths' fayre, the greatest in these parts & Tom [Browne's grandson] should have had a sight thereof, butt that it have proved so very raynie wether' (**4**, 133). St Faith's Fair originated about 1100 and continued until 1872. First a sheep fair and by the seventeenth century a sale for Scottish cattle brought down from Scotland by Highland drovers to fatten on the Norfolk marshes, the wide verges along many of the roads near Horsham St Faith today were for the sheep and cattle to graze on their way to market. Parson Woodforde described it as also 'a very large Fair for all Things'.

At the Norwich and Norfolk (St Faith's) Crematorium Sir Thomas Browne is depicted on one of five glass panels of famous Norfolk persons in the *porte-cochère* erected at the entrance to the Chapel of Remembrance in 1961. Designed by J. Chaplin and executed by E. F. Woods, Browne's depiction is especially apposite in view of his *Hydriotaphia or Urne-burial* with its account of the 'Solemnities, Ceremonies [and] Rites of . . . Cremation' (1, 140).

34 *The Gunton portrait of Browne, a contemporary painting by an unknown artist.*

Hunstanton
In a postscript to a letter written in 1653 to Sir Hamon L'Estrange of Hunstanton Hall about the treatment of his bladder stone, Browne asked, 'Sr, I pray at your leasure doe mee the honor to informe mee how long agoe the spermaceti whale was cast upon your shoare, & whether you had any spermaceti in any other part butt the head' (4, 286). The skull of this whale survived at Hunstanton Hall into the present century but exists no longer.

King's Lynn (Lynne, Lin)
Browne did much original work on fishes found in Norfolk and three observations relate to King's Lynn. 'A *pristes* or *serra* [*Pristis antiquorum*] taken about Lynne . . . answers the figure in Rondeletius . . . *Sturio*, or Sturgeon, so common on the other side of the sea about the mouth of the Elbe, come seldome into our creekes, though some have been taken at Yarmouth & more in the great Owse by Lynne' (3, 418). 'A small kind of smelt in shape & smell like the other, tak[en] in great store by Lynne & called primmes' (3, 430).

Lowestoft (Lestoffe), Suffolk
Browne's younger son, Thomas, a naval officer, served with distinction in the action fought off Lowestoft in 1665 when the Dutch fleet was defeated. Charles Harbord, elder brother of the purchaser of Gunton Park (q.v.) in 1676, also took part in this action.

Marlingford
In the chancel of its parish church is a memorial to 'Richardus Clarke Generosus, Medicus & Pharmacopeus praesantissimus, utpote magne illius apud Norwicenses Aesculapy Thomae Browne Equitis Aurati fidus minister et Comes.' Dr Richard Clarke who practised from Marlingford died in 1682 aged fifty-one years; Browne recorded that they dissected a dolphin together and on another occasion that he gave Clarke a badger's skull (4, 123, 189).

Mileham
From this now long and straggling village Dame Dorothy Browne's family originated; there are records of the family of Mileham in the 'Domesday Book'.

Newmarket (Newmarkett), Suffolk

'The King [Charles II] is at Newmarket [1680] & hath good wether for his Races and falconrie: divers go from hence to bee touched', (**4**, 165). The long-standing practice of touching by the monarch for the cure of tuberculosis, that Browne recommended for his patients, was discontinued in the reign of Queen Anne.

North Burlingham (Burlingham)

Dame Dorothy Browne's family of Mileham originated from the Norfolk village of that name (q.v.) and had moved to Burlingham by the sixteenth century (**3**). The family lived in the Parish of Burlingham St Peter whose church is now a ruin and not in use and Dame Dorothy Browne was baptised in this church on 17 February 1621.

Norwich (35)

Among Browne's many accounts of Norwich life his description of the Parliamentary Election of 1679 is one of the most evocative. 'Sr John Hobart and Sr Neville Catelyn . . . were caryed in chayres about the markett place after eleven a clock, with trumpets and torches, candles being lighted at windows, and the markett place full of people. . . . I could not butt observe the great number of horses which were in the towne, and conceave there might have been 5 or 6 thousand. . . . Wine wee had none butt Sack and Rhenish, except some made provision thereof before hand, butt there was a strange consumption of beere and bread and cakes, abundance of people slept in the markett place and laye like flocks of sheep in and about the crosse' (**4**, 104–5).

Heigham, now a ward of Norwich City, was in the seventeenth century a village outside Norwich on the banks of the Wensum and often figures in Browne's writings – he refers to it as a 'suburbe' of Norwich. Browne's barrister friend Sir Justinian Lewyn resided there, another friend and his first biographer, the Reverend J. M. N. Whitefoot was Rector of Heigham and in what is now the Dolphin Inn, Old Palace Road, Browne attended the ailing Bishop Joseph Hall after his eviction by the Puritans from the Bishop's Palace in 1643.

Norwich's contemporary remembrance of Browne is marked by the formation in 1946 of its Sir Thomas Browne Society by Eaton (City of Norwich) School and the naming of the library at the Norfolk and Norwich Hospital the 'Sir Thomas Browne Library' in 1978.

35 *Norwich Castle with the City of Norwich in the background, early eighteenth century. The Norman keep was the County Gaol from 1220 to 1887 when it was sold and converted to a museum. Browne took John Evelyn to visit the Castle in 1671.*

THE SOUTH-EAST VIEW OF NORWICH CASTLE.

To Sr Edmund Bacon Bart & Armine Wodehouse Esqr.
Knights of the Shire for the County of Norfolk.
This PROSPECT is gratefully Inscrib'd by their most Oblig'd humble Servt. Saml & Nathl Buck.

THIS Castle suppos'd to have been built in ye beginning of the Saxons & afterwards repaired, if not re-edifyed by Hugh Bigod Earl of Norfolk when he joyned with Prince Henry Son of K. Hen. 2 against his father.

Browne Quotations

'There is musicke even in beauty, and the silent note which Cupid strikes, farre sweeter than the sound of an instrument. For there is a musicke where-ever there is a harmony, order or proportion' (1, 84).

'But the iniquity of oblivion blindely scattereth her poppy, and deals with the memory of men without distinction to merit of perpetuity. Who can but pity the founder of the Pyramids?' (1, 167).

'All places, all ayres make unto me one Countrey; I am in England, every where, and under any meridian' (1, 70).

'There is surely a peece of Divinity in us, something that was before the Elements, and owes no homage unto the Sun' (1, 87).

'Charity begins at home, is the voyce of the world' (1, 77).

'Upon my first Visit I was bold to tell them who had not let fall all hopes of his Recovery, That in my sad Opinion he was not like to behold a Grashopper, much less to pluck another Fig' (1, 102).

'Life is a pure flame, and we live by an invisible Sun within us' (1, 169).

36 *The Buccleuch miniature by an unknown artist.*

'Man is a Noble Animal, splendid in ashes, and pompous in the grave' (1, 169).

'But the Quincunx of Heavens runs low, and 'tis time to close the five ports of knowledge' (1, 226).

'Though Somnus in Homer be sent to rowse up Agamemnon, I finde no such effects in the drowsy approaches of sleep. To keep our eyes open longer were but to act our Antipodes. The Huntsmen are up in America, and they are already past their first sleep in Persia' (1, 226).

'Let thy Studies be free as thy Thoughts and Contemplations, but fly not upon the wings of Imagination; Joyn Sense unto Reason, and Experiment unto Speculation, and so give life unto Embryon Truths, and Verities yet in their Chaos' (1, 261).

Oxnead

Only one wing remains of the splendid mansion where Charles II and Queen Catherine of Braganza were entertained by Robert Paston, first Earl of Yarmouth, on their Norfolk visit in 1671. Browne was also a visitor to the mansion and shared with the first Earl an interest in curious information and foreign countries.

Reedham

'*Corvus marinus*, comorants, building at Reedham upon trees, from whence King Charles the first was wont to bee supplyed' (**3**, 403). Cormorants, *Phalacrocarax carbo*, have been rare breeders in Norfolk during the present century but recently have become increasingly abundant as winter visitors to the Great Yarmouth area.

Swaffham (Swaffam)

'A white, large, and strong billd fowle, called a Ganet, . . . whereof I met with one kild by a greyhound neere Swaffam' (**3**, 402).

Thetford

'K[ing] James [I] came sometimes to Thetford for his hunting recreation but never vouchsafed to advance twenty miles further [to Norwich]' (**3**, 143).

Winterton

Browne communicated to the Royal Society in 1667–68 an account of a fossil bone exposed by the sea's erosion of a cliff at Winterton (**3**, 350).

Acknowledgements

Illustration nos 5, 6, 12, 17, 20, 24, 25, 28, 29 Norwich Central Library; 1, 14, 15, 34 Church of St Peter Mancroft, Norwich; 7, 13, 19, 35 Norfolk Museums Service; 30, 31 Norwich Health Authority; 36 His Grace the Duke of Buccleuch and Queensberry, KT; 11 T. C. Eaton and the Norfolk Record Office; 23, 37 Norfolk Record Office; 17 the Dean and Chapter, Norwich Cathedral; 3 Church of St Andrew, North Burlingham; 2 National Portrait Gallery; 4 Treasurer, Royal College of Physicians of London; 10 N. Spencer.
Grateful acknowledgement is made of a generous gift from the Viscount Mackintosh Charitable Trust towards the cost of publication.

Bibliography

Batty Shaw, A, 'Sir Thomas Browne's Meadow', *Notes and Queries* NS **18** (1971), 295–9.
'Sir Thomas Browne: the man and the physician', Vicary Lecture 1977. *Annals of the Royal College of Surgeons of England*, **60** (1978), 336–44.
Bennett, J. *Sir Thomas Browne A man of achievement in literature* (Cambridge University Press, 1962).
Browne, Sir Thomas *Sir Thomas Browne's Works including his life and Correspondence*, ed. S. Wilkin, 4 vols (London, Pickering; Norwich, Fletcher, 1835–6).
The Works of Sir Thomas Browne, ed. Geoffrey Keynes, 4 vols, new ed. (London, Faber and Faber, 1964).
Religio Medici and Other Works, ed. L. C. Martin (Oxford, Clarendon Press, 1964).
Eade, Sir Peter 'Sir Thomas Browne', a paper read in 1894, in *Collectanea De diversis rebus* (London, Jarrold, 1908), pp 121–38.
Finch, J. S. *Sir Thomas Browne A Doctor's Life of Science and Faith* (New York, Schuman, 1950).
Huntley, F. L. *Sir Thomas Browne A Biographical and Critical Study* (Ann Arbor, 1962).
Bishop Joseph Hall 1574–1656: A biographical and critical study (Cambridge, Brewer, 1979).
Jewson, C. B. *Simon Wilkin of Norwich* (Centre of East Anglian Studies, University of East Anglia, 1979).
Ketton-Cremer, R. W. 'The Visit of King Charles II to Norfolk' in *Norfolk Portraits* (London, Faber and Faber, 1944), pp 9–21.
Keynes, Sir Geoffrey *A Bibliography of Sir Thomas Browne*, 2nd ed. (Oxford, Clarendon Press, 1968).
Mardle, Jonathan (Eric Fowler) *Broad Norfolk* (Norwich, Wensum Books, 1973).
Osler, Sir William 'Sir Thomas Browne', *British Medical Journal*, ii (1905), 993–8.
Sharp, Rev. D. M. *The Church of St Peter Mancroft, Norwich* (Norwich, Jarrold, 1978).
Stephen, G. A. *Three Centuries of a City Library* (Norwich, The Public Library Committee, 1917).
Southwell, T. *Notes and Letters on the Natural History of Norfolk. More especially on the Birds and Fishes from the MSS of Sir Thomas Browne* (London, Jarrold, 1902).
Tildesley, M. L. *Sir Thomas Browne His Skull, Portraits and Ancestry*, Biometrika **15** (1923) 1–76 and published as a monograph of the same title.
Williams, C. 'The Pedigree of Sir Thomas Browne' *Norfolk Archaeology* **15** (1902–4), 109–13.
Souvenir of Sir Thomas Browne (Norwich, Jarrold, 1905).

Reference numbers of quotations in the text refer to the volume and page number of Geoffrey Keynes' *The Works of Sir Thomas Browne* (1964).

ISBN 0 9548964 0 8
Printed in Malta by Gutenberg Press

37 *Entry, dated 1666, in the Vellum Book of donations to Norwich City Library, recording Browne's gift of Justus Lipsius' works and, in a different hand, a volume of his own works. Both these donations by Browne are now in the Central Library Norwich, successor of the Norwich City Library.*

Norfolk Dialect

In a tract entitled *Of Languages and particularly of the Saxon Tongue*, Browne provided the first written record of the Norfolk dialect. 'It were not impossible to make an Original reduction of many words of no general reception in England but of common use in Norfolk, or peculiar to the East Angle Countries; as, Bawnd, Bunny, Thurck, Enemmis, Sammodithee, Mawther, Kedge, Seele, Straft, Clever, Matchly, Dere, Nicked, Stingy, Noneare, Feft, Thepes, Gosgood, Kamp, Sibrit, Fangast, Sap, Cothish, Thokish, Bide owe, Paxwax' (**3**, 80). Some of these were obsolete by the time Robert Forby's *Vocabulary of East Anglia* was published in 1830, but as the late Jonathan Mardle (Eric Fowler) wrote in 1973 others are still current Norfolk or words known to him, for example 'bunny' (for a bruise or swelling), 'mawther' (for a woman or girl), 'seele' (in 'I gave him the seal o' the day'), 'stingy' (meaning cruel or mean), 'thepes, thapes or fapes' (meaning green gooseberries), 'sibrits' (banns) and 'paxwax' (the sinew in a joint of meat). Browne also made the first mention in literature of the Broads (**3**, 426).

Browne's Dormitive

'We tearme sleepe a death . . . so like death, I dare not trust it without my prayers, and an halfe adiew unto the world, and take my farewell in a Colloquy with God.

> *The night is come like to the day,*
> *Depart not thou great God away.*
> *Let not my sinnes, blacke as the night,*
> *Eclipse the lustre of thy light.*
> *Keepe still in my Horizon, for to me,*
> *The Sunne makes not the day, but thee.*
> *Thou whose nature cannot sleepe,*
> *On my temples centry keep;*
> *Guard me 'gainst those watchfull foes,*
> *Whose eyes are open while mine close.*
> *Let no dreames my head infest,*
> *But such as Jacobs temples blest.*
> *While I doe rest, my soule advance,*
> *Make my sleepe a holy trance:*
> *That I may, my rest being wrought,*
> *Awake into some holy thought.*
> *And with as active vigour runne*
> *My course, as doth the nimble Sunne.*
> *Sleepe is a death, O make me try,*
> *By sleeping what it is to die.*
> *And [down] as gently lay my head*
> *Upon my Grave, as now my bed.*
> *How ere I rest, great God let me*
> *Awake againe at last with thee.*
> *And thus assur'd, behold I lie*
> *Securely, whether to wake or die.*
> *These are my drowsie dayes, in vaine*
> *Now I do wake to sleepe againe.*
> *O come that houre, when I shall never*
> *Sleepe [thus] againe, but wake for ever!*

'This is the dormitive I take to bedward; I need no other *Laudanum* than this to make me sleepe; after which I close mine eyes in security, content to take my leave of the Sunne, and sleepe unto the resurrection' (**1**, 89–90).

Back cover: *Statue of Sir Thomas Browne, Hay Hill by H. Pegram, RA (1862–1937) and the Church of St Peter Mancroft. Browne holds a shard of pottery in his right hand; the pedestal of grey granite is shaped to depict an urn. In Norwich there is also a privately owned miniature of the statue.*

ISBN 0 9548964 0 8

9 780954 896409